# The Easter St

**by Jan Holdstock**
Narration by Alison Hedger

Suitable for Key Stages 2 + Lower 3

For performance in schools and churches

**The Biblical Easter story retold with seven new songs and an improvised whole tone piece for the children to perform**

Approximate duration 25 minutes

## MUSIC

| | | |
|---|---|---|
| Song 1. | Procession! | *Three parts* |
| Song 2. | The Last Supper | |
| Song 3. | Garden Of Gethsemane | *With recorders* |
| Song 4. | We Want Barabbas | *Four parts* |
| Song 5. | On The Road To Calvary | *Possible soloist and audience response* |
| Instrumental Interlude – | The Crucifixion | *Whole tone piece* |
| Song 6. | Joseph Of Arimathaea | *Possible soloist or small group* |
| Song 7. | The Easter Story | *Two parts with recorders* |

A matching tape cassette of the music for rehearsals and performances is available, Order No. GA11085, Side A with vocals included and Side B with vocals omitted.

Pupil's Book Order No. GA11084 contains the narration, song words, choir and recorder parts


A division of Chester Music Limited
8/9 Frith Street, London W1V 5TZ

Order No. GA11083

ISBN 0-7119-7561-2

**The narration giving an account of the Biblical Easter story is to be found in the Pupil's Book**

# 1 PROCESSION!

**Three parts**

*Cue: "Hosanna in the highest!"*

**Brightly** ♩ = 120

Bdim7 A D G
rides on His way. Here He comes on the don - key. Hail to Je - sus.
D D/A A7 D
Hail, Mes - si - ah you are wel - come to - day. 2. Ho - san - na in the
G D Bdim7 A/C♯
high - est. Bles - sed is He that comes in the name of the Lord. Ho -
D G D
- san - na in the high - est. Bles - sed is He who comes to preach the

D/A A7 D G D Bdim7 A
ho - ly word. 3. Palm branch - es wave. The peo - ple shout and cheer.
D G D D/A A7 D
Palm branch - es wave to show the world our Sav - iour's here.
div.
(no chords) D D/C♯ D/B D/B♭ A
Part 1
1. Here He
Part 2
2. Ho -
Part 3

D
G
comes on the don - key.
Hail to Je - sus.
- san - na in the high - est.
Bles - sed is
3. Palm branch - es wave.
The
D
B^dim7
A
Hail, Mes - si - ah as He rides on His way.
Here He
He that comes in the name of the Lord.
Ho -
peo - ple shout and cheer.
D
G
comes on the don - key.
Hail to Je - sus.
- san - na in the high - est.
Bles - sed is
Palm branch - es wave
to

1st time
D
D/A
A7
D
Hail, Mes - si - ah you are wel - come to - day. Here He
He who comes to preach the ho - ly word. Ho -
show the world our Sav - iour's here.
2nd time
D/A
A7
D
(no chords)
A7
D
wel - come to - day.
ho - ly word.
Sav - iour's here.
f

# 2 THE LAST SUPPER

*Cue: The time for Jesus to fulfil the scriptures was getting closer and closer.*

D7 G C6
one more time. We've done it all be - fore but it's diff - 'rent to - night.
Slower ♩ = 110
G D7add2 G B Em
rit.
Some - thing's not right. 1. Lord, why must you wash our feet?
2. Lord, why must you go a - way?
rit.
F♯dim7 G7/F Em7 E♭aug5
We don't un - der - stand. But
And what shall we do? For
C/D G/D D♭dim7 D7/C G D7/A D7
(Refrain) tempo 1
you are the Mas - ter. We'll do what you com - mand. It's
you are the Mas - ter. We're no - thing with - out you.

Final Refrain
G C6 D
good to have a meal with all your friends a - round you. Sit - ting at the ta - ble with the
G C G
folk you know. Shar - ing the food, shar - ing the wine,
Slower ♩ = 110
A A7 D7 G/B A♯dim7 D7/A E7
shar - ing the com - pa - ny one more time. But ever - y - thing's new. Ever - y - thing's strange.
Am Am7 D7 G
No - thing will ev - er be the same a - gain.

# 3 GARDEN OF GETHSEMANE

**With recorders**

*Cue: "Couldn't you keep watch with me for just an hour?"*

* *This melody note F♯ is different from the G used in the third bar of the introduction*

A7 Em7 F# Gmaj7 G
on - ly the pale star - light.
trem - ble with ice cold fear.
We must stay a -
D Em Bm
- wake for the Mas - ter's sake.
A7 D G Bm Em Bm
Keep sleep from our eyes un - til the sun - rise.

# 4 WE WANT BARABBAS

**Four parts**

*Cue: " . . . We want Barabbas – set Barabbas free!"*

Dm Am7 Dm Am7 Dm Am7
Part 1
We want Ba - rab - bas! Set Ba - rab - bas free! Je - sus is guil - ty!
Part 2
We want Ba - rab - bas! Set Ba - rab - bas free!
Part 3
We want Ba - rab - bas!
f
Dm Gdim7/A Dm Gdim7/A
Cru - ci - fy him! Cru - ci - fy him! Cru - ci - fy him!
Je - sus is guil - ty! Cru - ci - fy him! Cru - ci - fy him!
Set Ba - rab - bas free! Je - sus is guil - ty! Cru - ci - fy him!
Part 4
We want Ba - rab - bas! Set Ba - rab - bas free! Je - sus is guil - ty!
Dm Gdim7/A Dm
unison
All: Cru - ci - fy him! Cru - ci - fy him!
ff

# 5 ON THE ROAD TO CALVARY

**Possible soloist and audience response**

*Cue: All three were to be crucified together.*

Em/B Bm Em Am/E Em7 Am6 Em Am
road to Cal - va - ry.
To see their friend and preach - er.
His jour - ney to the moun - tain.
King Je - sus who is pass - ing.
On the
Em/B Bm Em Am/E Em7 Am6 Em Am
road to Cal - va - ry.
Their preach - er and their heal - er.
The moun - tain full of sad - ness.
Is pass - ing to Gol - go - tha.
On the
1.2.
To finish
Em/B Bm Am/E Em Am/E Am6/E E
rit.
road to Cal - va - ry.
-ry.
rit.

Play the instrumental interlude in any of the following ways.

1) Play the tune on recorders or sing it to ‘ah’. Play the accompaniment on the piano.

2) Play the tune on recorders or sing it to ‘ah’. Play the accompaniment on tuned percussion or other available instruments. The bottom part is a repeated G so you could use the open string of a violin, viola, cello or guitar.

3) Create your own tonal poem using the whole tone scale.

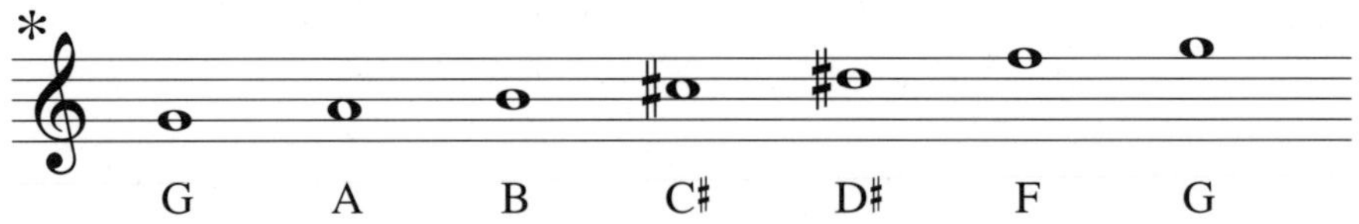


The advantage of this scale is that all the notes fit, whatever order they are played in! Each child’s part can be very simple – one or two notes will do. The children must be aware of all the other players and no one part should dominate. A single sound unit should be created from many individual components. Experiment with dynamics and differing tonal qualities of various instruments and playing at different octaves. Introduce non-pitched percussion as desired, if it is decided that they add to the desired atmosphere.

* *There are no semitone intervals as found in the conventional major and minor scales. The nature of a whole tone piece is unusual and creates an ethereal and atmospheric feel.*

# INSTRUMENTAL INTERLUDE
# THE CRUCIFIXION

### Whole tone piece for recorders and other available instruments

*Cue: Jesus had died on the cross.*

# 6 JOSEPH OF ARIMATHAEA

**Possible soloist or small group for first verse**

*Cue: Guards were placed at the entrance.*

B♭6 D Gm D
I have a fine tomb set in the rock face.
Now all is ov - er, the pain of death is past.
Gm Am/G F/A Dm F/C C C7 F
Sealed by a boul - der, in a ho - ly place.
Here in the gar - den He can rest at last.
Coda
F B♭6 F B♭/C F
mp

# 7 THE EASTER STORY

## Two parts with recorders

*Cue: " . . . Truly, I am with you always, for ever and ever."*

B♭ E♭6 Cm F/C C7 F
Recorder
B♭ E♭ B♭
Vocal descant with repeat v.1 only
Sing Hal - le - lu - jah, sing Hal - le -
1. This is the Eas - ter sto - ry. The stone is rolled a -
2. Ma - ry came to the gar - den. She found the tomb was
3. "Look at my face" said Je - sus. "I am a - live a -
Repeat 1. This is the Eas - ter sto - ry. The stone is rolled a -
F B♭ E♭
(With repeat v.1 only)
- lu - jah, sing Hal - le lu - jah.
- way. Je - sus is ri - sen in glo - ry.
bare. "Where have they ta - ken my Je - sus?"
- gain. Now I can come to my king - dom,
- way. Je - sus is ri - sen in glo - ry.

Refrain
F
C7
F
F7
B♭
Recorder
Recorder (third and final time)
(With repeat v.1 only)
Hal - le - lu - jah.
Part 1
Hal - le - lu - jah,
div.
Part 2
Ri - sen for us to - day.
She asked the gar - d'ner there.
for ev - er - more to reign."
Ri - sen for us to - day.
Hal - le - lu - jah,
E♭6
F
Gm
D
(Recorder)
(Part 1)
spread the news. Sing of peace and love. For
(Part 2)
spread the news. Sing of peace and love. For

Cm/E♭ F7 B♭ F Gm7 Cm/E♭ F7 B♭
Je - sus has ri - sen for ev - ery - one. Glo - ry to God a - bove.
Je - sus has ri - sen for ev - ery - one. Glo - ry to God a - bove.

Coda
Cm/E♭ Gm/E♭ F/E♭ E♭add2/F F B♭
Glo - ry to God a - bove.
Glo - ry to God a - bove.
rit. cresc. al fine

# Also by Jan Holdstock

## for Key Stages 2 and 3

### A Christmas Welcome

Jan Holdstock

The Christmas Nativity story retold through narration and seven attractive songs for junior choirs, Church groups and all those who love to sing. The songs can be sung alone or performed together as a cantata. Alternatively, mime or a play can be added to create a Nativity.

Teacher's book GA11028
Pupil's book GA11029
Matching tape cassette GA11030

### In Viking Times

Jan Holdstock

Ideal for cross-curricular Key Stage 2 Viking projects: an all-year-round musical presentation with six songs in unison, two and three parts plus narration. Illustrations of Viking characters are included which will stimulate costume ideas and the teacher's book contains useful 'Did You Know' facts.

Teacher's book GA11035
Pupil's book GA11036
Matching tape cassette GA11037

### Footprints on the Moon
**Apollo 11**

Jan Holdstock

The true story of the first landing on the moon retold in narration and five new songs, plus recorder parts. Can be performed as a concert piece or used as a musical framework for a historical space drama.

Teacher's book GA11053
Pupil's book GA11054
Matching tape cassette GA11055

# The Easter Story

**by Jan Holdstock**
Narration by Alison Hedger

The Biblical Easter story with seven new songs

PUPIL'S BOOK
Contains the choir and recorder parts,
narration and song words

The Teacher's Book, Order No. GA11083, contains the piano score,
vocal lines, instrumental parts and chord symbols

A matching tape cassette of the music for rehearsals and performances is also available,
Order No. GA11085, Side A with vocals, Side B with vocals omitted.


A division of Chester Music Limited
8/9 Frith Street, London W1V 5TZ

Pupil's Book Order No. GA11084

ISBN 0-7119-7562-0

# 1 PROCESSION!

## Three parts

comes on the don - key. Hail to Je - sus.
- san - na in the high - est. Bles - sed is
3. Palm branch - es wave. The
Hail, Mes - si - ah as He rides on His way. Here He
He that comes in the name of the Lord. Ho -
peo - ple shout and cheer.
comes on the don - key. Hail to Je - sus.
- san - na in the high - est. Bles - sed is
Palm branch - es wave to
1st time
Hail, Mes - si - ah you are wel - come to - day. Here He
He who comes to preach the ho - ly word. Ho -
show the world our Sav - iour's here.
2nd time
wel - come to - day.
ho - ly word.
Sav - iour's here.

# 2 THE LAST SUPPER

# 3 GARDEN OF GETHSEMANE

## With recorders

# 4 WE WANT BARABBAS

## Four parts

# 5 ON THE ROAD TO CALVARY

## Possible soloist and audience response

Instrumental Interlude

# THE CRUCIFIXION

**Whole tone piece for recorders and other available instruments**

Gently ♩ = 80

# 6 JOSEPH OF ARIMATHAEA

**Possible soloist or small group for first verse**

Gently ♩. = 88

# 7 THE EASTER STORY

## Two parts with recorders

Refrain
Recorder (third and final time)
Hal - le - lu - jah.
Part 1
Hal - le - lu - jah,
div.
Part 2
Ri - sen for us to - day.
She asked the gard - 'ner there.
For ev - er - more to reign."
Ri - sen for us to - day.
Hal - le - lu - jah,
(Recorder)
(Part 1)
spread the news. Sing of peace and love. For
(Part 2)
spread the news. Sing of peace and love. For
Je - sus has ri - sen for ev - ery - one. Glo - ry to God a - bove.
Je - sus has ri - sen for ev - ery - one. Glo - ry to God a - bove.
Coda
Glo - ry to God a - bove.
Glo - ry to God a - bove.

**It was just before the Passover when crowds of people followed Jesus on his way to Jerusalem. Jesus sent two of his disciples on ahead to the next village where they would find a tethered donkey with its colt. "Untie both animals and bring them here to me" said Jesus. "If anyone asks what you are doing, just say "The Lord needs them". So the disciples did as Jesus asked and brought him the donkey and colt. Jesus got up onto the donkey and rode it into Jerusalem. The crowds greeted him and threw their coats and tree branches along the way. They shouted, waved and chanted:**

> **"Hosanna to David's son!"**
> **"Blessed is the one who comes in the name of the Lord!"**
> **"Hosanna in the highest!"**

## 1. PROCESSION!

*Each verse is sung in order, then voices divide into three parts and sing three verses simultaneously through twice.*

*1.*

Here He comes on the donkey. Hail to Jesus.
Hail, Messiah as He rides on His way.
Here He comes on the donkey. Hail to Jesus.
Hail, Messiah you are welcome today.

*2.*

Hosanna in the highest.
Blessed is He that comes in the name of the Lord.
Hosanna in the highest.
Blessed is He who comes to preach the holy word.

*3.*

Palm branches wave.
The people shout and cheer.
Palm branches wave
To show the world our Saviour's here.

**As Jesus sat with his twelve disciples at supper, he knew his time on earth was running out. He got up from his place, took off his outer clothing, wrapped a towel around his waist and began to wash his friends' feet, wiping them with the towel. "You rightly call me your Teacher and Lord" he said. "As I have washed your feet and made myself lower than you, so too must you do likewise for each other. I have washed your feet as an example."**
**Jesus then put his outer clothing back on and resumed eating. The time for Jesus to fulfil the scriptures was getting closer and closer.**

## 2. THE LAST SUPPER

*Refrain*

It's good to have a meal with all your friends around you.
Sitting at the table with the folk you know.
Sharing the food, sharing the wine,
Sharing the company one more time.
We've done it all before but it's diff'rent tonight.
Something's not right.

*1.*

Lord, why must you wash our feet?
We don't understand.
But you are the Master.
We'll do what you command.

*Refrain*

It's good to have a meal . . .

*2.*

Lord, why must you go away?
And what shall we do?
For you are the Master.
We're nothing without you.

Final *Refrain*

It's good to have a meal with all your friends around you.
Sitting at the table with the folk you know.
Sharing the food, sharing the wine,
Sharing the company one more time.
But everything's new.
Everything's strange.
Nothing will ever be the same again.

**Judas, one of Jesus' twelve disciples, had previously left the supper table early, as he intended to betray Jesus to the authorities. After supper, Jesus and the remaining eleven disciples went to the garden of Gethsemane. Jesus asked Peter and two others to come along with him to a secluded place, to keep him company whilst he prayed. This they did and Jesus went on a little further and earnestly prayed "Father, if it is at all possible I would rather not go through with the coming ordeal – but your will be done, not mine." He then returned to his friends and found them sound asleep. "Peter" he said, "Couldn't you keep watch with me for just an hour?"**

## 3. GARDEN OF GETHSEMANE

*1.* In the garden of Gethsemane
We must watch and pray through the night.
All around is darkness
With only the pale starlight.
We must stay awake for the Master's sake.
Keep sleep from our eyes until the sunrise.

*2.* In the garden of Gethsemane
There is danger now always near.
All our hope has left us.
We tremble with ice cold fear.
We must stay awake for the Master's sake.
Keep sleep from our eyes until the sunrise.

**Judas led a group of soldiers and officials to the garden where he guessed Jesus could be found. Jesus met them and asked " Who are you looking for?" "Jesus of Nazareth" they replied. "Here I am" said Jesus. They arrested him and tied him up and took him away to Annas for questioning. Whilst Jesus was still tied up he was sent to Ciaphas, the high priest. But he too was unable to find a good reason to keep Jesus under arrest. So in the early morning Jesus was taken to the Roman governor, Pontius Pilate. By now an angry crowd had gathered and Pilate declared "I find no basis for making charges against this man. But I have been advised by Ciaphas your high priest, that it is the Jewish custom to release one prisoner at Passover time. Would you like me to release Jesus?" The crowds shouted back at Pilate, "No! Not that Jesus man! Release Barabbas. We want Barabbas – set Barabbas free!"**

## 4. WE WANT BARABBAS

*This song is sung in unison, then each of the four parts enters in sequence as in a round. The last line "Crucify him!" is repeated until the fourth part has also sung this line. There is then one more final unison "Crucify him!"*

We want Barabbas!
Set Barabbas free!
Jesus is guilty!
Crucify him! (*repeat line – see above*)

Crucify him! (*unison*)

**Pilate wanted to let Jesus go, so he again appealed to the crowds. But they kept shouting "Crucify Jesus! Crucify! Crucify!" Pilate eventually agreed to comply with the crowd. He let Barabbas the murderer free, and handed Jesus over to the mob. Two other criminals were led out at the same time. All three were to be crucified together.**

# 5. ON THE ROAD TO CALVARY

*The verses could be taken by soloist. The response "On the road to Calvary" which comes at the end of every line, could be sung by the audience/congregation.*

*1.* The crowd is still and waiting.
*On the road to Calvary.*
They're waiting there to see Him.
*On the road to Calvary.*
To see their friend and preacher.
*On the road to Calvary.*
Their preacher and their healer.
*On the road to Calvary.*

*2.* Two common thieves are with Him.
They're with Him on His journey.
His journey to the mountain.
The mountain full of sadness.

*3.* The people shout Hosanna.
Hosanna to King Jesus.
King Jesus who is passing.
Is passing to Golgotha.

**It was now midday and darkness covered the whole land for three hours. The temple curtain tore in two, the earth trembled and shook, and Jesus called out in a loud voice "Father – I commit myself to you." Jesus had died on the cross.**

## INSTRUMENTAL INTERLUDE – The Crucifixion

*A whole tone piece which could be sung to "ah" or played on any suitable instrument.*
Ideas are given in the Teacher's book, p.16.

**In the evening a rich man called Joseph of Arimathaea sought permission from Pilate to take Jesus' body down from the cross and put it in a place of rest. Pilate agreed and so Joseph wrapped Jesus in linen and placed him in an unused tomb cut out of the rock face. Joseph rolled a large boulder over the entrance and went away. The chief priest and Pharisees went to Pilate and requested that the tomb be made more secure so that no one could enter and remove Jesus' body. Pilate agreed and the boulder at the tomb entrance was sealed with ropes and clay. Guards were placed at the entrance.**

# 6. JOSEPH OF ARIMATHAEA

*First verse could be a solo or a group of voices.*

*1.*

Please let me help you.
Give Jesus to me.
I know the right place
For Him to be.
I have a fine tomb
Set in the rock face.
Sealed by a boulder, in a holy place.

*2.*

Please let him help you.
What he says is right.
Jesus needs somewhere
To stay tonight.
Now all is over,
The pain of death is past.
Here in the garden He can rest at last.

**It was now the first day of the week and Mary and Mary Magdalene went to Jesus' tomb hoping to anoint his body, although they hadn't any idea how they could possibly remove the boulder. When they got there, there was a tremendous earth tremor and an angel appeared, shining like glistening snow. He rolled the stone away from the entrance and sat upon it. The guards fell down in a faint. The angel spoke to the women and told them Jesus was no longer in the tomb but he was alive again. "Mary" said a second being whom she thought was the gardener. But at the sound of his voice she instantly knew this was the risen Lord Jesus! The excited and joyful women ran off to tell the eleven disciples that Jesus was alive and walking about. When Jesus came to his disciples he said the following to reassure them, "I have been given all authority in heaven and earth. Always remember what I have taught you and make disciples of every nation. Truly, I am with you always, for ever and ever."**

# 7. THE EASTER STORY

*Recorders play introduction and again before each verse. They also play the descant melody to the third and final Refrain.*

Sing Hallelujah,
Sing Hallelujah,
Sing Hallelujah,
Hallelujah.

1\. This is the Easter story.
The stone is rolled away.
Jesus is risen in glory.
Risen for us today.

*Divide into two parts for Refrain:*

*Refrain* Hallelujah, spread the news.
Sing of peace and love.
For Jesus has risen for everyone.
Glory to God above.

2\. Mary came to the garden.
She found the tomb was bare.
"Where have they taken my Jesus?"
She asked the gardener there.

*Divide into two parts for Refrain:*

*Refrain* Hallelujah, spread the news . . .

3\. "Look at my face" said Jesus.
"I am alive again.
Now I can come to my kingdom,
For evermore to reign."

*Divide into two parts*:

*Refrain*+recorder Hallelujah, spread the news . . .

*Keep two parts and sing repeat of verse one with vocal descant simultaneously as follows:*

| | | |
|---|---|---|
| *Repeat* 1. | This is the Easter story . . . | Sing Hallelujah, |
| | The stone is rolled away. | Sing Hallelujah, |
| | Jesus is risen in glory. | Sing Hallelujah, |
| | Risen for us today. | Hallelujah. |

*Final Refrain*+recorder Hallelujah, spread the news. . .

*Coda* Glory to God above.



ISBN 0-7119-7562-0

GOLDEN APPLE PRODUCTIONS
A division of Chester Music Limited
PUPIL'S BOOK ORDER NO. GA11084